Poetic Conscientious

A Journey for Motivation and Spiritual Growth

Glenandre Rollins

First Edition

NEWMAN SPRINGS PUBLISHING
320 Broad Street
Red Bank, NJ 07701

First originally published by Newman Springs Publishing 2024

ISBN 979-8-89308-478-8 (Paperback)
ISBN 979-8-89308-479-5 (Digital)

Printed in the United States of America

Christian Spiritual

In Him Is the Cure

Bad things will happen
In spite of what we think
things beyond our control
that leaves us helpless and weak.

Unable to speak a word
No comfort can be reached
A dark cloud surrounds us
so the pain cannot be breached.

Until the moment that we *seek*
help from far above the sky
In Him we place our hopes and fears
No more question of the how and why.

For weeping may endure for a night
but joy will come in the morning
God is saying "It's okay to cry"
but to trust in His love brings the glory.

Christian Spiritual

Heavenly Heartbeat

A heavenly heartbeat
i s a *measure* beyond
any feeling you may seek

It perpetuates
all acts of kindness
to be good to others, with good deeds

To the children that you feed
from the change given
to the beggar on the street

A heavenly heartbeat
is the source of
the unconditional love, we all need.

Love Has Feelings Too

Love hates to be ignored
Love hates to be unkind
Love hates to be forbidden
mostly because love is blind

Love likes to be shared
Love likes to be there
Love likes in the moment
beyond words to compare

Love takes time to show
Love needs time to grow
Love creates a type of bond
stronger than glue can hold

Love is tamed and unique
Love is often bitter sweet
Love is the reason *God* has made
me for you and you for me.

Redemption Comes with a Price

The price of redemption
equals love, multiplied by
forgiveness, divided by trust,
then subtract the pain.

The sum of the total,
is the cost of salvation.
A debt replacement,
to clear my name.

My level of greatness.
My destiny's changing.
My head held high,
as I display my hat.

It took some time,
but I was patient.
My self-respect,
I've now earned back.

A Touch Above

Maybe we were meant to be
a touch above extraordinary.

A love so pure, it's naturally sweet
creation chosen us, for the world to *see*

Like two love birds, sitting high in a tree
"I for you and you for me"
meaning our love will last eternity.

Perfect Is He Who Saves Me

They say a man is not supposed to cry
It's almost like an 11th commandment.

So why then? Do I swim in a river of tears
when I feel hurt, lost and abandoned.

With a current so strong at times
it threatens to take me under.

I persevere through determination
which serves to make me stronger.

Does this make me any less of a man?
Of course not! it means I'm a human being,

Created with emotions which is a DNA from God's
genes.

So, if Jesus wept, than so can I.
He was the perfect example of a man,
who wasn't afraid to cry.

Through Faith the Lord Is Praised

Faith is not a small measure
of what we trust in or believe.

Faith has a huge bearing
on what we can do and achieve.

Without faith, one is destined to fail
With the wrong type faith, one is destined for hell.

I speak for the faith, in the Almighty One
the creator of everything, who sent only begotten *Son.*

He has inspired my faith, to sit and to write this poem
I believe He done so, not for me but so other may get
to know Him.

So I pray today, that His message was properly conveyed
But don't clap for me, for it is the Lord who is worthy
to be praised.

His Creation

We are his creation,
and our being here
is an example of His glory.

We are His servants,
our job is to learn
and to spread His story.

We are His children,
for Him to raise
as He so please.

Yet He allows us to have
free will, for us to choose
to follow His lead.

Our wonderful counselor, Gracious Host
Almighty King of Kings.

Our Heavenly Father is undoubtedly
our truest friend indeed.

Cosmic Love

A star has heat and light
far about this world to achieve.
We can only marvel at its beauty
from a distance, and make a wish if you believe.

You are my star here on earth,
you create for me the light I need.
With a passionate heat inside you,
you keep me as warm as can be.

My wish is for us to be
together both now and forever.
To create our own galaxy of stars
'cause in your love I found heaven.

Count Once Again on Love

How many ways, is it to say,
"I love you?"
because once is not enough.

I have searched far
but could not find
another with your special touch.

Your intellect captivates my mind,
your style stimulates my lust.
Your beauty is one of a kind,
I treasure the Aura between us.

It is a passionate connection,
that is precise and sincere.
You are the center of my affection,
I feel overwhelmed when you're near.

You are truly the sweet and precious, love of my life.
There are three words in "I love you,"
but you're one in a million in my sight.

Live Consciencely

Your conscience is your
inner voice of reason.
Think of it as your personal GPS
that will guide you,
when skepticism blurs your vision.
It holds the power of persuasion,
which is used for the greater good.
More often than not, you will regret,
not listening to it when you should.
So take heed to its warnings
and it will keep you in good health.
Your conscience is there to help you
and to protect you, from yourself.

The Truth about a Lie

A lie is destructive
it is just as effective
as death.
The real difference is
you'll still be around,
to regret what was said.
Every reason for a lie
is to hide the truth.
Every truth behind a lie
threatens to expose the real you.
So take the road less traveled
and step on up to the plate
because unlike death
it's not over
but it very well
maybe too late.

Christian Spiritual

This Thing Called Life

Life can be a blessing as well as a curse,
It all depends on how you think about it.
In this world there are many struggles and hardships
but life as we know it, cannot, exist, without it.
Here we have air, land, water and food,
the main ingredients for our survival.
Try living without these necessities,
you'll find the need, for some help, to revive you.
As beautiful as the world may be, we still take it for
granted.
It is the only place we were made to live,
with peace and love as *God* commanded.
Yet we still fight amongst ourselves,
with wars over religion, race or colors.
We are all part of the human race,
so that makes you my sisters and brothers.
As it is, I can't wait to leave this earth,
death holds many mysteries to be desired.
I'm speaking of revelations, the *new* heaven and Earth
where no more tears, will be, required.

Hope Not Despair

Faith is like the air,
you can't *see* it.
Although, it is something
you desperately *need.*
A blind Man, cannot
see the sunshine,
but he can definitely
feel its beam.
Love is invisible,
and it takes time to grow.
without it, one will feel empty.
with it, the love will clearly show.
Nurture your faith,
protect it, as if it
depends on your very life.
walk with, grow in
your faith, so that
you'll spend Eternity
in the light.

Deep Cleansing

Inside of me, there is a feeling
unexplainable in words
but clearly seen, through my spiritual healing.

I am not the person, that I used to be.
My change process, was a hard lesson to learn,
because I was a prisoner to my reality.

Now that the Lord's will,
has found its way into my heart.
God's purpose has been revealed,
and has created for me, a new start.

One Walk in Christ

There are five deadly venoms,
as well as seven deadly sins.

With another six thousand ways to die.

There is but one way, to be born again.

Conscious Motivational

Potential to Be

Every person has potential to be,
something beyond the ordinary.

You possess a talent,
and within you lies the key.

To unlock doors,
to unlimited possibilities.

Each Reason Leads to Purpose

Every person has a reason,
Every reason leads to purpose.

Do not forsake who you are,
by compromising your life service.

You were created to do a job,
with this life you were granted.

Your mission is to fulfill your destiny,
Even when it's beyond your understanding.

Every person has a reason,
Every reason leads to purpose.

I hope not to forsake who I am,
by compromising my life service.

I was created to do a job, with this life I was granted.

My mission is to fulfill my destiny, even when it is beyond my understanding.

The Physiology of You and Me

The Physiology of you and me
defines the *essence*
beyond what the eyes can see.

A reality created by words
of emotions,
filled with warmth and harmony.

"To be or not to be,"
in love with you,
is not the question.

Meaning there is not,
a single doubt,
that inside your love
I found heaven.

Essence of Poetry

The essence of poetry means to *me*,
words that move you mentally not physically.

These are words to be used,
as food for thought.

Helping you to remember things you should do,
from the things you ought not.

So feed your soul to *ease* your mind,
you will find peace more often,
that will last a lifetime.

Elevate to the Afterlife

Life is like an Elevator Ride
it is full of ups and downs, you'll find.

Ironically so is death
but it has only one destination in mind.

Infinity, Immortal, Eternal; are words that means everlasting.

They have a beginning, but Elusive is the point of passing.

Death in the physical form is chartered
by these three words alone.

It is now for you to decide
which ride with death
shall you forever call home.

Over the Years

Looking back over the years
I shed more than just tears
I shed old skin
I shredded relationships
from family to friends.

Growth was mandatory process
both natural and insistent
Humbling my mind, body and soul
creating a *new* definition for my existence.

Beginning the final chapter
to a long and drawn-out story.
My purpose, my morals, my success
Reveals the Almighty's heavenly glory.

Men of Generation X

My brothers, my brothers; what have we done?
We have forgotten the ways of old,
Now the next generation is all about having fun.
They think what they see on TV,
Is the way that life ought to be.
They think a woman's size of her,
breast and her butt is her reality.
Not caring about her attitude, career, goals or personality.
How has making fast money,
Driving fast cars, and meeting fast women,
Become more important than career jobs, saving money,
And independent living?
I see something wrong, very wrong,
And it saddens me to say.
Our community is becoming a trend,
And
It too shall one day fade away.

Thank You

Thank you for taking the time,
to get to know me.

Thank you for being there,
to hold and console me.

Thank you for loving me,
truly and unconditionally.

Thank you for sharing your world,
with me; exclusively.

Thank you for all the things,
that you say and do.

I thank you mostly,
for just; being you.

Touched

I love the way you,
talk to me; because you never demanding.
I love the way you,
listen; with a full understanding.
I love the way you,
massage; all my tension and pain.
I love the way you,
caress; away my sorrows and blame.
I love the way you,
fill me; with a pure desire.
You move me in more ways,
than words can inspire.
With just your walk and style,
I become undone.
I love the way you touch *me*,
in more ways than *one*.

Fatal

Make no excuses
I'll make no exception.

Toying with my love
it's like playing with a deadly weapon.

I'm serious about my love
make no mistake about it.

It's like the air I need to breathe
I cannot live without it.

So look, but don't touch
don't even speak
there is *no need.*

For once you become
a threat to my love
things become fatal indeed.

The Quality of High Esteem

I marvel at your
ability to be.
Awe-inspiring
both total and complete.

A shining example
for others to *seek*.
Majestically inclined
both complex and unique.

A style o radiant
it automatically transcends.
A genuine original
so hard to pretend.

How grateful am I
to call you a friend.
With such sophisticated demeanor
from beginning to *end*.

Our Destiny Is Written

Ambition is what drives us,

our choices, are what leads us to it.

Fate and Destiny, is the divine plan.

Meaning the outcome, wasn't ours,

to choose it.

Commitment to Forgiveness

Who Am I to you?
a Criminal?
a sorry individual? one
whom has done you wrong?

What then, will make amends?
for things I've said or did; to
restore peace, back into your home?

I now have realized,
to have apologized,
wouldn't be sincere enough,
for me to give.

So, I opened my heart
took out all of the parts
were evil and deception
once lived.

As for replacement
there is love, joy and
patience, suitable enough
for the Almighty to dwell.

And forgiveness was placed,
through mercy and grace.
now my new Destiny is
heaven not hell.

Fundamentals of Trust 101

Trust has many variables
and communication is the key.
Find someone you're comfortable with
in which, openly you can speak.

Step one, you have to let someone in.
you have to give a little
to receive a lot,
in order to begin.

Step two, allow yourself
to say what's on your chest.
it is up to the listening person
to stand up to the test.

Step three,
They would give a sound advice,
and be a shoulder you can depend.
Be thoughtful of your feelings, enough
not to run and tell their friends.

A Father's First Day OTJ

I would like to rewind,
the hands of time,
back to when it first all began.

Was so long ago,
the day I knew for sure,
I had finally become a man.

With such a sweet sensation,
my heart was racing,
my body was pouring sweat.

It was then that I knew,
as the day grew,
it would be one I'll never forget.

I waited for the sign,
until labor was done,
as the situation became calm.

Was to my surprise,
as she opened her eyes,
to see the proud father,
I have become.

A Wonderful Place to Dance

Rainbows and lollypops,
fairy tales and seashells.

A world full of magic,
where beautiful music,
fills the Air.

A Palace for our love,
where Daughters Dance
with Daddies too.

I'll take the stars
out of the sky,
'cause they don't shine,
bright as you.

The Remedy Me = Self-control

I now control my level of stress,
now that I understand four pertinent keys.
I have always been successful,
just only at doing the wrong things.

I tried to change the way I felt,
'cause feeling normal was so lame.
So I used so much for so long,
it became normal to feel that way.

I was blessed with having less,
and yet still that was ok.
There was no fuel for my ambition,
for the decisions I had to make.

I had to stop compromising,
willing to spend, rather than save.
I had to become useful to others,
and push my selfishness away.

I had to stop
looking around corners,
trying to find
someone else to blame.

I had to search
deep within myself,
to find the *errors*
that needed to change.

Love's Eminent Decline

The fact that I'm writing
instead of sitting, next to you,
leaves only one implication.
I have been detained
somewhere, too far for a
face to face conversation.
I must have lost my mind,
misplaced it, thrown it away,
along with my common sense.
I should have known time
and space would change things,
and your presence would be missed.
I never pictured a life without you,
you with someone *new*.
Life goes on I guess.
What do I do with this feeling
about a love, I cannot forget?
I'm at a loss for words, so I'm
ending this now, although the way
I feel I cannot change. I
realized you were the "*one*" I lost,
and my selfishness is to blame.

Keep Me O' Lord

Mirror me, in your image o' Lord
martyr me, if it to be thy will
Strengthen me, with your favor o' Lord
least the evil within, shall over spill.

Cover me, with your mercy o' Lord
deliver me, from all this pain
This war has become too much o' Lord
to endure without your grace.

Place me, among the angels o' Lord
so I may sing all day your praise
Embrace me, completely with your love
so never again shall I, be afraid.

Skeptic Identity

I have a radical disposition
little to no comprehension
for people's expectations of me.

I feel no appreciation
for my current situations
no one else to blame but me

Not looking for some pity
just need someone who really
wouldn't mind to help a brother in need

Just need some ventilation
without stipulations
somebody to lend a hand
when I can't reach.

Alienated Suspicions

Bad company breeds
bad character,
bad character brings distain.

No one wants to be
the bad apple,
that gets left out, in the rain.

Tossed out like the trash,
cause you might
spoil the whole bunch.

Separated from
family and friends
who claim to love you so much.

Thrown down like the litter
to deteriorate and wither,
left alone by yourself
without a love to consider.

Christian Spiritual

Until Then

Weary is the brokenhearted,
bereaved are those in mourning.
Sadness consumes the present,
when a loved one moves on to glory.
At peace is where one resides,
once they take leave of this place.
We will rejoice in the knowledge,
of knowing one day, we shall see their face.
Ascending into the House of the Father,
where again, next to them we will stand.
Together forever in the presence of the Almighty,
we shall sing (songs of praise) and we will dance.

The Day I Never Saw Coming

Mom

Today is the day
that your heart will break
the clouds will thunder
and the earth will quake

Today was the day
that time stood still
no oxygen to breathe
constant pain will kill.

Today was the day
the world stop revolving
no time to decipher
fiction from reality

Today was the day
I surely lost my mind
already lost my will
because I lost my mom.

Dad

Today is the day
that your heart will break
the clouds will thunder
and the earth will quake

Today was the day
that time stood still
no oxygen to breathe
constant pain will kill.

Today was the day
the world stop revolving
no time to decipher
fiction from reality

Today was the day
I lost what the strength, I had
nearly lost my sanity
because I lost my *dad*.

A Variety of Adoration

A bouquet creates
a symphony
as Roses and Lilies
build harmony.
Camellia and Jasmine
sings melodies.
Blue bonnets and Lilacs
have a wonderful smell,
as do Irises, Magnolias
as well as Laurels.
A beautiful combination
to set on display,
this one is for you
on this Mother's Day.

Happy Mother's Day!

Momma Said

Momma said
The value of my life
isn't based on the money I have
And
The love I will receive shouldn't
change the person I am.
Momma said
Don't try so hard to be liked
be original and let it show
And
True love isn't hard to find
its pure magic that'll make you glow.
Momma said
Trust your first intuition
and it will lead you well and
save your money for rainy days then
you won't experience a dry spell.
Momma said
I love you child, listen close
and everything will be okay.
Then I said
I love you too Mom, and
Happy Mother's Day!

Maw Maw: Granny's

Happy Nana's Day!

Mothers are really wonderful
they are so "*great*" that
inevitably they become "*grand*".

They are the cornerstone
of creation, where girls
become *women*, boys become *men*.

Grandmas take special care
to spoil the children, then
send them straight back to mom.

This is done out of love
for the child, plus a little
payback is out of fun.

All in all, Grandmas are
the best. They have all
the qualities of Mom, without
none of the stress.

Happy "Mother" of my Mommy's Day!

Brilliant Essentials

You have the
power to create
endurance to achieve
skill to motivate
faith to believe
patience to wait
the need for speed
knowledge to stop
with a will to succeed.
So whatever it is
that you decide to do
all the power needed
lives inside of you.

Thought Observations

No one ever gets
into trouble for just
thinking bad things

When that thought
becomes *an* action,
is when the confusion, start to begin.

Saying or doing those
thought, entice others
to feel a certain way.

It may create a
reenforced action
that'll leave you in dismay.

So think twice before you act
especially before you speak.

You will receive a response.
just maybe not the *one* you *seek.*

Conscious Motivational

Courage and Faith Overshadow Fear

I am aware that I often make mistakes,
I'm unaware of all the problems that they may create.
I am aware that my fears will often hold me back,
I'm unaware of all the opportunities I miss because of
the courage I lack.
I am aware to gain knowledge is vitally important,
I'm unaware of my future, I just hope not to blow it.
I am aware of the commitments I must make, to take
a chance of life, with one huge leap of

Faith…

Magnificent Persuasion

I Love You, the mother
to our beautiful baby girl.

I respect you, the *woman*
who deals with my crazy world.

I Thank you, for more
than I have room to say.

But I wish for you the best
and Happiest Mother's Day…

Anonymous Prosperity

Think good thoughts, it will determine the things you say.

Speak good things, it shall determine the things you do.

Do good, for it will develop int a habit.

A habit of good will sharpen your character.

And your character will determine your Destiny.

—Unknown Author

When We Meet Again

W hen we meet again
the sight of you
will bring me joy.
No hesitations
No limitations
No more separations
to endure.
Once you're in my arms
I'm going to steal your breath away,
I will embrace you
with my love
and kiss your lips
until no words
you're able to say.
When we meet again
I'm going to take control completely,
I will lay you down
melt away your tension,
erotic perfection
leaves no protection
only thrills and intensity.
When we meet again
I'll be going all in
sheer pressure

from the pleasure
ending shock waves
To origins deep within.
once I find your treasure
I'll bring it to full release.
exposing true passion
raw emotion
liquid ecstasy
that will leave you
floating on a dream.

First Impressions

Getting to know you
is my pleasure
I value more than wealth

Getting to touch you
is a privilege
I want all to myself

Getting to taste you
Humm, so sweet
I can hardly wait

Like a desert I enjoy
I'll eat the whole damn plate

Touch me tease me
if you only dare
I'll capture your heart
with a smile
that will make your inhibitions disappear

Truest Expression of Love

God bless you, Although; you didn't *sneeze.*
He has placed you in my life, with such perfect qualities.
God has blessed me, of course; by sending me a queen,
One whom I can cherish from her crown down to her feet.
You're genuine and driven, open-minded amongst other things.
A faith-based believer in Christ, the Lord of Lords—King of Kings.
You are supportive of my decisions, yet you hold me accountable I must say.
You encourage me to stand tall, by the strength that you display.
Your expectations are high, creating for me a standard I have come to love.
Your concern for my well-being is matched only from above.
I have a passionate lust for you only, for you complete me in every way.

My seeking eyes has been immobile, for your beauty
is here to stay.
Your breathtakingly beautiful, the true first love of
my life.
I thank *God* each day that I've found you, and have
made you my wife.

New Beginnings

You taught me something
about myself, I never knew before.
you showed me a desire
which urges me to explore.

You created for me a passion
be it lust or love
I don't know.

But we became both
open and willing
to see just how far
this feeling can grow.

Be it now or forever
I'm willing to take the chance.

What started out with a smile
could end up a true romance.

Either Now or Forever

I must confess to you my love,
I can't afford to wait a minute.
Unless, I wish to suffer the rest,
of my life without you in it.
I am determined to be persistent,
cause there is no time to be wasting.
Under any other circumstance,
my approach would be subtle and patient.
I have a passionate obsession,
that is precise and sincere.
You are the joy of my affection,
I feel overwhelmed when you're near.
Here I am standing, wishing, praying,
that you will accept my hand in marriage
and forever by my lady.

Love Half Past Gone

Things may change
as time will tell
speaking of a love
I once knew so well.

Mistakes were made
time was lost
and love was
soon to follow.

Be as it may
how I feel today
still no love remains
for tomorrow.

Insatiable You

You create in me a desire,
unlike anything I felt before.

It is like a passionate heat,
that burns hotter than the *sun's core.*

My satisfaction is nearly impossible,
because I could never get enough of you.

Your love is astounding,
taking me beyond the depths of the deep blue.

Be it the sky or the ocean,
your love is uncharted territory;
for me to search seek and find.

A single man on a single voyage,
means any and all discoveries are mine.

Conscious Motivational

Determined and Destined to Succeed

When your best is not enough,
it is easier to accept defeat,
than it is to roll up your sleeves,
and not give up.

In time you'll learn to fight,
even until your untimely death.
Giving 110 percent of everything,
your very best until your last breath.

Let's face it, who's keeping tabs anyway,
your success to failure ratio is proof,
you will live to see another day.

Your reward lies just around the corner,
you just have to make it there to see.
But if you quit now,
then who would know
just how great you could be.

Susceptible to Change

Change is inevitable, and time is most certainly to blame.
Be it people places and things,
they are all subject to change.

Even the weather changes in *season*,
when you break a dollar you'll receive change.
No matter how you chose to look at it,
nothing *ever seems* to remain the *same*.

So be flexible and expectant because
change is coming, this I know.
It is sure to change the way you live,
in a way that may help you grow.

Angel Wings

When you take the time to listen,
you can hear the most peculiar things.
If you focus the *noise* in the distance,
you may hear the sound of Angel wings.

They are sent here for our protection,
for direction, amongst other things.
They were sent by His discretion,
for we are conceited human beings.

Angelical beings are marvelous wonders,
you and I are His greatest creations.
He even sent to us a part of Himself,
because our souls were worth saving.

We are to treat each other well,
with love and kindness as He so deemed.
On this pathway to enlightenment Angels are here to,
guide us the way we need.

Parallel of Enlightenment

Inspired by a song…

I finally know where He is.
The Lord I've been trying
So desperately to find.
And all of this time,
He has been very near.
He is always around me,
And His word is clear.
If I spend my time
With Him every day.
Then I'll learn that
He's perfect in all
Of His ways.
I've been looking
For the Lord, and
He's right here with me.
If I look in the mirror,
I would see He lives
Right inside of me.

Analyze the Disguise

Most personalities are simple to read,
others can be rather complicated.
Some attitudes are consistent it seems,
while others are continually, changing faces.

Some people focus on the external of things,
the walk, talk, and style of dress.
Most of which is superficial it seems,
because what's beneath describes you best.

Not trying to be judgmental I mean,
to make aware to you a skeptic's forte.
It will alert you of their deceptions,
also protect you from the games they play.

Same Struggles Different Solutions

I've found an underwater mountain
and it's the biggest I've ever *seen*
It is just like any other mountain
except it is underneath the *sea*.

It has ridges, sloes and mounds
all the way up to its peak
It would be nearly impossible
to climb, because there is no gravity.

This mountain you'll have to swim
and as easy as that may *seem*
You will find this still impossible
especially without oxygen to breathe.

Although a mountain is still a mountain
they are not all the same
There will exist many dangers
It's your approach that needs
to change.

Persona of Extravagance

A fine glass of wine
of potent Eloquence and
sophistication.
Your beautiful like a
Red rose with a
versatile temptation.
Such a hypnotic
persuasion of exotic
sensations.
The "Crème de la crème"
from all across the nations.
VVS—the best, facets,
you're a diamond quality.
A standard above the rest
'cause that's what you are to me.

Living Today to Better Tomorrow

Yesterday is a memory
thoughts of the past
feelings have come and gone.
Any business left unattended
sadly must remain undone
Today is a present
an opportunity for change
such a beautiful gift to behold.
A chance to be courageous
through determination and by being bold.
Tomorrow is not promised
neither are my future expectations.
In order for my survival
I must prepare a plan
for my future obligations.

The Center of Gravity

Lost in the whirlwind,
A drift into outer space.
I'm foreign in my homeland,
No recognition of this place.

So tossed between decisions,
To press on or let go.
I use motivation for ammunition
'Cause inside me there is a war.

It is cold out here alone,
I need some shelter from the rain.
I knocked on doors I used to know,
No one's home to let me in.

Again I have to realize
I'm all alone by myself.
I have nothing left to lose
Except my pride and my health.

I'm determined to maintain,
Because I'm destined to succeed.
Through persistence to achieve
My mission, I can do anything
If I believe.

Freedom to Be Me

When I look outside myself,
the world is what I see.
I wonder what the world would be like
if the world was just like me.

Full of lots of emotions like,
love, joy, hope and peace.
No fear of confrontations
’cause I have no enemies.

No need for segregation,
’cause we are all one family.
Will lend a hand, no hesitations
because we live in harmony.

What such big dreams I’m chasing,
some expectations hard to reach.
This world would be amazing
if it had could be, just like *me*.

Christian Spiritual

Change Me, Lord

I listened to myself as I opened my mouth to speak. I didn't sound like myself, so I asked the Lord to change me. I spoke of women, not how my mom had raised me. I spoke of not having a job, that made me sound lazy. I took a look at myself, and I looked kind of crazy. My hair was growing out, and my clothes were kind of holey. If I hadn't known any better, I would swear I didn't know me. I stood on my feet, but I was going nowhere slowly. I reached out to the Lord, and this is what *he* told me.

Repent, repent, repent! Because your life is full of sin. You're wallowing in self-pity, that's why my light cannot shine in. Your faith in me is weak. On bended knees is where you begin. Ask the father for forgiveness, it would be His grace that He will send. Right before my face, I felt a change in me take place. He renewed my sense of purpose and self-esteem along with faith. I now see through the devil's lies disguised as shame, guilt, and depression. I'm so glad to know the Lord, His faithful Love and all His blessings.

Absolute Resiliency

In this Life, many times
we shall fail, we will fall.
What matters the most
is persistence not perfection,
To get up and stand tall.
setbacks and road blocks
mean to divert our motivation.
To disable and discourage us,
to rethink our situation.
In order to bounce back,
we have to trust and believe.
Trust that in time things
will get better and believe
That someday, we shall succeed.

Christian Spiritual

Designed to Illuminate or Illuminate by Design

You are part of a plan,
of one big grand design.
A role meant just for you,
revealed only in due time.
Destined to leave your mark,
on the life you left behind.
Continuing an unsung legacy,
that your influence helped to decide.
No expectations for you to perform
don't have to memorize any lives
Just embrace life for the moment
You're living righteously, will provide.
Now is the time to be courageous.
from this drama you cannot hide

World's Greatest Dad

There are so many qualities to describe,
my warrior, my hero, my friend.
But the title I love the most,
would be "The world's Greatest Dad."

My hero, does take the risk,
even if it means his very life.
Willing to go above what's necessary
in order to achieve what is right

My friend, does lend a helping hand,
and is eager to listen with precision.
He is a shoulder I can depend on,
helping me to make wise decisions

My Father, is there to steer me well
with reliable and good direction.
He has raised me with integrity and honor
and provided me with complete protection.

My Dad to me, you're all of these things
for this you are loved and well respected
You have always been consistent
so I always know what's expected

How blessed Am I, to have such a guy,
to teach me to grow and become a man.
I pray one day, I'll be half as good
as the world's Greatest Dad.

Essentially Made for Me

To truly express
what you mean to me,
Go far beyond words.
So I must define,
your qualities.
You are genuine and driven
amongst other things.
A strong believer in Christ
the Lord of Lords, King of Kings.
So irreplaceable you are,
my true and best friend.
So incredible you are,
so much more than amazing.
Your love is the glue,
That binds our family
through thick and thin.
Your considerate of others,
meeting their needs
Before yours begin.
I'll never forget
how you nursed me,
until I was back to health.
Giving of your time
effort and energy,

having little to none
left for yourself.
You have always been the one
on whom I could depend.
You were always there for me to talk to
about almost anything.
Undoubtedly your love provides,
the strength that carries me.
I know for sure, that
your love is the cure.
And that it is all I need.

Aspire, Acquire, Adapt

In an imperfect world,
I strive for perfection.
A boundless compassion,
that spirals into obsession.
My will, often contradicts
the choices I make.
Leaving endless speculation
is this my doing or is this fate?

I remember I must
forgive to be forgiven,
such a risky proposition;
where I surrender
in order to win.
After the damage is done,
is there room for growth and
improvement? Staring
in the face of adversity
I insist
to push to get through it.

The Paradox of Consciousness

Simplicity is the measure
of our serenity.
To improve our appreciation
for our fantasies and
exaggerations.
We submit
to a truth beyond our
understanding, with a
reality beyond our
imaginations.

Who Is God?

He is the air we breathe.
He is the breeze in the trees.
He is exactly what we need.
He is the sun that shines
light on my heart. He keeps
me as warm as I can be.
He is the water we drink,
He keeps me hydrated and clean.
He is the Earth from which
I grow, where He raise
the food so I can eat.
He is the Word, He is
the Truth that it speaks.
With a breath alone He
has made everything that
we see.
He is the Alpha and Omega,
the beginning and the End.
He is the Creator, My Savior
and truly my Best Friend.

Spontaneous Revitalization

I'm not broken, just damaged at best,
it depends on the current perspective.
I've been wounded by missed opportunities,
been paralyzed by constant rejection.
My independence and self-sufficiency,
Relies on society's, denial or acceptance.
That the system has altered my thinking,
until my behavior was properly adjusted.
No provisions to form a solution, so I am open to any
suggestions.
My intuition is not so vivid, so I'm vulnerable and feel
kind of desperate.
I am prompted by my ability, to envision a new direction.
To stimulate the ingenuity, inside me,
that contributes to my perfection.

Tremendous Obligation, Observation and Gratitude

Father's Day Represents,
a sacred bond between
you and I.
You have shown me the
true value of things,
that will help me to grow
throughout life.
You are my prized
Possession, your loyalty
is one of a kind.
Exceptional are your
values, always willing
to spend quality time.
You taught me that pride
Will take me nowhere,
being humble will keep me
where I need to be.
Your love is so unconditional,
not because I'm lovable, rather
because; you are so loving.

You have even loved me
the most, when I
deserved it the least.
Your discipline was always
just, making sure proper
correction was received.
Willing to say no to my
wants, so to provide me
the things I need.
Instilling the priority of
character, willing to earn it,
instead of spoiling me.
Even though I mess up,
I take pride in the way
you have made me.
Because of you, I'll be
a better person
hopefully as incredible,
as the one who raised Me.
Happy Father's Day!

Encrypted Disposition

I welcome the Adversity
that awaits me.
For it shall bring *new*
challenges my way.

Armageddon, and act
of fate.
I look forward to
seizing the day.

My fascination is chaos
and confusion.
Provokes a perfect
opportunity.

Redefining the moment
to stimulate,
A confidence into
my ingenuity.

For every crisis
there is a cure.
Analyze the conclusion,
to find the deception.

You will find out
there is a clue to
create a balance
to make the corrections.

Suggestive Reasoning of Prestige

A beautiful assassination
means to me, to sacrifice
my wants out of compassion
for the things you *need*

To be absolutely selfless
by my actions, accountable
for the things I say, by
being compelled to do good deeds

Living a life that matters
means to inspire a brilliant
motivation by a combination of
enduring love and bold ambition

Flying above what is required
to blaze a trail on wings of
fire. Being confident and
strong-willed, exceptionally composed
with superb precision

A beautiful assassination
means to sacrifice my wants
out of compassion for your *needs*

Being absolute and accountable
for my actions and words,
compels me to do good things

Living lies that matter
inspires motivation of enduring
love and bold ambitions

Flying high on wings of fire
going above what's required,
confidently composed with
pure intentions

Appropriate Persuasion of Authentic Sensations

I have learned when I lack
what others may have,
this makes me even more special.
Becoming superficial over trivial things,
creates a competition for your affection.

You are good to me, your good for me
there are no other ways around it
you absorb the Romance inside me,
completely inside out, it increases
the quality of the technique,
that erases all of my doubt.
Your love inspires and motivates *me*,
to become that type of *man*.
Who will hold open your door,
and delights in holding your hand.
Willing to converse my sentiments of love,
while watching the sun set into the view
someone who will pay close attention, and listen to you,
about all of your hopes and fears.
I'll provide the solutions for your tension,
and be a shoulder for your tears.

You entice me, so exciting,
your love invites me to be all that I am.
It is because of you, being a part of life
that I am, a better Man.

Precious Impressions

Sparkles of light, so brilliant in color

When I envision a butterfly, I think of my Mother.

So beautiful in flight, above the rays of the sun

No other feels as right, Her love is second to none.

I pray for one day we might, spread our wings and fly together

Into the blue sky's unknown, all the way to Heaven.

Tribute to You

I hope/today, will go your way

I pray/you get, a birthday wish

May your wish/come true, I hope it do

Just remember my love, that I Love You

Happy Birthday!

Critical Chain Reaction

A man's life is a reflection
of his thoughts and actions
to the way He lives.

The cause and effect
creates a chain reaction
for the things that He did.

What you live by, you
will likely die by, it
is proven to be true.

A life of integrity and
service with faith and courage,
will in death lead to Respect and
honor with love for your purpose.

Motivational Poem

Bold Reasoning

Faith isn't something you see
trust in what you believe
and you will know

Courage is invisible
until you stand
it will not show.

You'll find there is a key
the key is to believe.

Then your faith can grow
and courage will show
to unlock the door to
unlimited possibilities.

Variety of Inspirations

To excel in excellence
you must first exceed,
all limitations.

To strive for perfection
you will succeed,
through determination.

Living your lives with purpose
will strengthen your motivation,
to overcome all your fears
in spite of your situation.

An Altered Configuration

Inspired by Ruff impression

I was lying to myself and *God*
my family and friends.
I once thought I had it all,
living in a dream full of sin.
Please don't be so quick to judge me,
'cause nobody is perfect.
Looking back I made mistakes
Now I see wasn't worth it.
Playing the hand I was dealt.
I should have folded the game.
Tossed away so many years
I must have been insane.
Had much promise as a kid,
you can believe it or not.
Thought it to be cool to keep on playing,
until the day I got caught.
Turned out it really was a blessing,
sitting there in disguise.
Had plenty of time for contemplation,
I finally opened my eyes.
The first time in my life,
I know exactly what to do.

I am committed to this fight,
don't have no time to lose.
Now I bow my head only to God,
not dodging bullets or gravels.
I choose to live my life this way,
because I want to not have to.
Please don't get the wrong impression, of me,
because of my past.
I am as capable of doing good,
as I was a good, doing bad.

I had to humble myself, in order to make
a change. My intuitions and intentions
helped to change the rules of the game.

A Reservation for Two

I hear today is your birthday,
and I pray you get whatever you wish.
I know today you'll be very happy
although, this day with you I will miss.

I tell everyone I know about you,
of how beautiful and wonderful you are.
About how your smile shines bright like sunshine,
and the twinkle in your eye look like stars.

Oh, how I miss all the silly fun we had,
the laughing the playing and dancing.
I look forward to being together again,
so we can enjoy the greatest picnic I'm planning.

There will be sandwiches, and fruit, cakes and pies,
such sweet tasting things sent from above.
Everything will be perfect made just right
because our secret ingredient is Love.

Marvelous, Majestic, Profound Energy

I'm inspired to believe,
the unbelievable things of my dreams.
Even though I'm unable to understand,
exactly what they all mean.
I aspire to excel in excellence,
for one day, I will soon achieve.
Just by being persistent and driven,
I am destined to accomplish many things.
I'm encouraged to live out my life.
Without being discouraged, in spite of my doubt.
I may struggle at time, but I'm willing to fight,
because that is what my mission is all about.
My determination came to be by faith,
meaning the motivation I need comes from above.
His will is perfect and divine plan for me,
that enables my endurance to thrive from His love.

About the Author

Born to Glenn Lee Mitchell and Gloria Jean Rollins in the year of our Lord 1979, date being May 16. At 5:59 a.m. started what would be a tale so made for the movies, on second thought, soon to become the creation of his next writing adventure. A life taken for granted, a child abused, bullied, neglected, and burned. Like the phoenix finding a way through the refining fire, being tempered, tried, and tested. Coming out stronger than ever, now finding purpose from the rubble of the past.

9 798893 084788

Printed at Repro India Ltd.